My Year

ROALD DAHL
MY YEAR

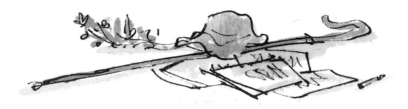

Illustrated by
Quentin Blake

JONATHAN CAPE
LONDON

JANUARY

WHEN I was a little boy, I had a tiny boat made of tin (there was no plastic in those days) which had a very small clockwork motor inside it, and I used to play with it while I was having my bath. One day the tiny boat developed a leak in its hull and it filled with water and sank. For many weeks after that, I would lie in my bath worrying about whether my own skin would develop a leak in it just as the little boat's hull had done, and I felt certain my body would fill with water and I would sink or die. But it never happened and I marvelled at the watertightness of the skin that covered my body.

Whether you are playing with a little boat or not, a hot bath is the best place for all of us in the miserable month of January. The excitement of Christmas is long past and school is soon beginning again and there is really nothing to look forward to except the cold weeks ahead. If I had my way I would remove January from the calendar altogether and have an extra July instead.

For the last twelve months we have all been living in one year and now all of a sudden it is another. It is extraordinary how this tremendous change takes place in the space of a fraction of a second. As the clock approaches midnight on the thirty-first of December you are still in the old year, but then all at once, one millionth of a second after midnight, you are in the new. I have always found this sudden change from one year to another awfully hard to get used to, and all through the new January that follows I keep writing down the old year instead of the new one on letters and cheques and other bits of paper. The same sort of thing happens on your birthday when you are nine years old one day and ten years old the next. It is lovely to be a year older, but it is the suddenness of it all that is so amazing.

January, I now remember, was the month when I had my first office job in London at the age of eighteen. The pay was five pounds a week and I used to travel up by train from where we lived in Kent to a station in the City of London called Cannon Street. As soon as I jumped off the train there was a mad gallop through the crowded streets in the slushy snow to reach the great hall of the Shell Company's building in order to clock-in by nine o'clock. I was one of a small group of Eastern Staff Trainees and absolute punctuality was demanded of us. If we were late, we were reported to the directors. At lunchtime I used to go to a pub for a pork pie and a beer, and on my walk back to the office I always, absolutely always, treated myself to a tuppenny bar of Cadbury's Dairy Milk chocolate. By the time I got back to the office I had eaten all the chocolate, but I never threw away the silver paper. On my very first day I rolled it into a tiny ball and left it on my desk. On the second day I rolled the second bit of silver paper around the first bit. And every day from then on I added another bit of silver paper to that little ball. The ball began to grow. In one year it had become very nearly as big as a tennis ball and just as round. It was extraordinarily heavy. When I picked it up it felt like a lump of lead and I think this was because in those days, some fifty years ago, the silver paper they used to wrap chocolate in was much thicker than it is today and very much superior all round. I never lost my chocolate-silver paper ball and today it sits, as it has done ever since I started to write, on the old pine table beside my writing chair. That table is now cluttered with many curious objects that have found their way on to it over the years. As I sit here in my comfortable chair with my writing board across my lap, I can see scattered over the table top the following things:

A baby seal carved out of whalebone, given to me by some Eskimos in Canada.
A meteorite the size of a golf ball.
A painted fragment of a small ancient vase picked up in a ploughed field in Greece.
A strangely shaped stone found in a river bed in Texas, made by Red Indians many years ago.
One of my own hip bones (the head of the femur) which the surgeon gave me after he had sawed it off and stuck a steel one into me instead. He said it was worth keeping because it was the biggest hip bone he had ever seen. A steel hip (called a prosthesis) is on my table too. This one was  once embedded in my body but it went wrong and had to be replaced. It is rather a beautiful object made of shining steel that looks like a Turkish dagger, and it has a little ball on one end.
A glass bottle full of mauve-coloured bits of gristle immersed in preserving fluid which another surgeon gave me after he had chopped them out of my spine.
A cone from a cedar tree. I love cedar cones.
A rough stone ball as big as a melon which has been cut in half to reveal very beautiful blue-veined agate inside.

Another glass bottle in which lies the tiny mechanism or valve which I helped to invent for draining off excess fluid from the ventricles of the brains of children who suffer from a type of brain injury known as hydrocephalus.

A Star of the Desert, which is a large and marvellously shaped piece of stone, crystalline and reddish-brown and crinkly all over. I picked that one up in the Libyan Desert during the war.

A large piece of ambergris preserved in a bottle. Look it up in the dictionary and you will see that it is the intestinal secretion of the sperm whale and is much prized by makers of expensive perfumes. It is found by beachcombers who often spend years combing the silver beaches in far-off Pacific Islands for this valuable and peculiar substance.

My father's silver and tortoiseshell paper-knife.

A marvellous carving of a green grasshopper sent to me by someone who had read *James and the Giant Peach*.

A transparent plastic box with a miniature musical box inside it which starts to play 'Edelweiss' as soon as you put it into the sunlight. This is just the sort of toy that fascinates me. No clockwork, no batteries, just let the sun shine on it and it plays you a tune.

A small model of a Hurricane fighter plane made for me by a boy who had read *Going Solo*.

A wonderful piece of rock veined with opal that glistens and glows in red and green and blue. It was sent to me by a young lad who lives in a place called Mintabie in the remote outback of Australia. Mintabie only exists because of the opals they find there, and when I was in Australia in 1989, I spoke by radio-telephone to the children of the tiny Mintabie school. To this particular boy, I said, 'Do *you* ever find any opals?' 'We all find them,' he answered, and apparently, as soon as he got the chance, he rushed down to the creek and hunted until he found this splendid specimen which he mailed to Puffin Books in Melbourne with a request that they forward it to me. Of course, I wrote to thank him.

A piece of stone with ancient cuneiform writing on it which I picked up in Babylon, of all places, during the war in 1940. Three other pilots and I hired an old car and drove miles across the Iraqi desert to visit this famous city. It was amazing and totally deserted. The streets and houses were all about fifty feet below ground level and the walls were covered in carvings of lions and mythical beasts. We wandered through the silent streets and among the ruins and I shall never forget the air of mystery and wonder that surrounded us everywhere.

Lastly, on my old table, there is a photograph of my lovely wife Liccy and another of my first granddaughter Sophie.

There is just one small bright spark shining through the gloom in my January garden. The first snowdrops are in flower.

FEBRUARY

IS February, we ask ourselves, any better than January? Well, yes, in a way it is because you know that if only you can get through it and put it behind you, then the worst of the winter is probably over. On the other hand, this is usually the fiercest and bitterest month of all. I treat February like a school term and keep counting how many days there are left until it is over.

All the same, there are a few small blessings here and there as the month goes by. You begin to see long yellow catkins forming on the hazel bushes. You hear the blackbirds starting to sing, and the magpies are beginning to patrol their territories. I don't like these clever cheeky magpies because they prey upon the nests of other birds. In April, they search out the carefully concealed nests of thrushes and blackbirds and all the smaller birds as well, and they either go in and steal the eggs or worse still, they watch and wait until the babies are hatched and then they swoop in and take them away to eat. I once stole a young magpie from the nest and tamed it and kept it for a couple of years as a pet. I never put it in a cage. That wasn't necessary. It stayed around all the time in the garden and would sit on my shoulder like a parrot. When I went for walks it would follow me the whole way

there and back, circling overhead, and when I woke up in the mornings, it would be sitting on the sill of the open window. Oh yes, you can tame a magpie quite easily if you get it young enough, but you mustn't ever trust it completely. It will peck suddenly at shiny objects. I knew a farmer the other side of Aylesbury who had his own tame magpie sitting on his hand and he was trying to teach it to talk. Suddenly the bird caught sight of a glint of light in the man's eye and stabbed at it with its long sharp beak. The farmer, who lived in Grendon Underwood and was called Richard Holt, lost the eye. He also got rid of the magpie.

Only once have I discovered a new molehill in our orchard in the month of February. I love seeing molehills because they tell me that only a few inches below the surface some charming and harmless little fellow is living his own private busy life scurrying up and down his tunnels hunting for food. But a mole seldom digs new tunnels in February. Autumn is the time when they do that because as the weather gets colder in October and November, the worms and grubs which the mole feeds on go deeper into the soil and therefore the little mole has to dig new and deeper tunnels to catch them.

Do you know anything about moles? They are remarkable animals. They are shy and gentle and their fur coats are softer than velvet. They are so shy that you will seldom see one on the surface. Each mole has his or her own private network of tunnels which are not much more than five or six inches below the surface, and the front paws of the little creature are shaped like huge spades to make digging easy. The molehills that you see are not of course their houses. They are simply piles of loose soil that a mole has pushed up out of the way because, after all, if you are digging an underground tunnel you have to put the excavated soil somewhere.

A mole can dig about three feet of tunnel in an hour and he usually owns about one hundred yards of his own private tunnelling which no other moles go into. All moles prefer to live solitary lives, each one trotting up and down his own network of tunnels day and night, searching for food. His food consists of worms, leatherjackets, centipedes and beetle grubs, and the fantastic thing is that he actually has to eat *one half of his own body weight* of these tiny delicacies every single day in order to stay alive! No wonder he is a busy fellow. Just imagine how much food *you* would have to eat to consume half your own body weight! Fifty hamburgers, one hundred loaves of bread and a bucketful of Mars Bars *and* the rest of it each and every day. It makes one quite ill to think about it.

The mole is not a very attentive husband. When mating time arrives, he simply burrows into the tunnel of a female neighbour, and after he has mated with her, he returns once again to his own territory, leaving his wife to give birth and rear the babies on her own. Mind you, we all know a few human males who behave in more or less the same way but let's not get into that.

Being a gardener myself, I have always regarded the mole as a friend because he eats all the horrid centipedes and leatherjackets and other pests that damage our flowers and vegetables. A lot of country people wage savage war against the poor moles because of the molehills they make, and they kill them in all sorts of cruel ways, using traps or poison or even poisonous gas. But I will tell you a very simple method of persuading a mole to leave your garden or your field. Moles cannot stand noise of any sort. It makes them even more nervous than they already are. So when I see a molehill in the garden, I get an empty wine bottle (plenty of those around our house) and I bury it in the ground close to the molehill, leaving only the neck of the bottle sticking up. Now when the wind blows across the open top of the bottle it makes a soft humming sound. This goes on all day and night because there is almost always some sort of a breeze blowing. The constant noise just above his tunnel drives the mole half-crazy and he very soon packs up and goes somewhere else. This is not a joke. It really works. I have done it often.

February, incidentally, is the month when female mosquitoes emerge from their winter hibernation to lay their eggs on slimy ponds. The males are all dead. They died in the autumn. And by the way, it is only the female mosquitoes that bite people. A curious and little-known fact such as this is worth tucking away in your memory.

MARCH

I RATHER like the month of March. I know it can be bit-
ter cold, but your heart is lifted by the signs of approach-
ing spring all around you. Halfway through the month most
of the hedges are covered with a pale powdering of green as
the little leaf buds begin to burst, and the pussy willows are
smothered in yellow pollen. Crocuses are flowering bril-
liantly in patches of white and yellow and blue around the
garden, and best of all, the nesting season is beginning to get
seriously under way. I can discover where four or five nests
are being built simply by watching through the windows of
my house. From the dining room, I can see a pair of blackbirds building ten feet up in the trunk of the big clipped yew
tree. From the sitting room, I watch a thrush carrying bits of
dry grass up into the branches of the vine that runs along the
west wall of the house. From the same place, I see a pair of
blue tits popping in and out of a small hole in the wooden tool
shed across the lawn, exactly as they did last year and the year
before. From the kitchen window, I see a pair of robins
making a mossy nest, more a hole than a nest, in the bank
underneath the heather-bed.

When I was a boy, I was an avid collector of birds' eggs. I
know it is forbidden now, but in those days nearly every boy

who lived in the country was a collector. When I took an egg from the nest, I used a teaspoon so as not to leave the human finger smell behind on the other eggs because this might make the mother desert. To blow the egg I made one hole only, using a small drill which I twizzled back and forth between finger and thumb. Then I took a stainless-steel pipette with a very thin curved end which was inserted ever so carefully into the single hole. Very gently, I blew through the pipette which forced the white and the yolk out of the same single hole. It was all very professional. Real egg collectors never make two holes, only one. I had a cabinet with a glass door and there were ten drawers in it. Each drawer contained a lot of square compartments, small ones for the tiny eggs and large ones for the big eggs. It was an enthralling hobby for a young boy and not, in my opinion, in the least destructive. To open a drawer and see thirty different very beautiful eggs nestling in their compartments on pink cotton wool was a lovely sight. And I could always remember vividly how and where I had found each and every egg. The wonderful deep olive green of the nightingale came from a nest with four eggs found one evening at the foot of an oak in the close of Llandaff Cathedral. The guillemot's egg, as big as a hen's egg and sky blue with black splashes, was discovered after a hair-raising climb up a cliff on Caldy Island off the Pembrokeshire coast, and I carried it all the way down the cliff again in my mouth. The sparrow hawk and the kestrel and the carrion crow all were gotten from the tops of very tall trees literally at the risk of life and limb. The list was long because I had one hundred and seventy-two eggs at the end of it all. Of course not every egg was from a different species of bird. There were eleven house sparrows' eggs, each with different colourings and speckles, and I even had a hen's egg that was as perfectly round as a large marble. The wren was the smallest of them all and the black-backed gull was, I think, the largest.

By the end of the month ladybirds are on the wing once again, and you will notice that nearly all of them are the two-spotted kind. Peacock butterflies and small tortoiseshells are emerging from their winter sleep, hunting for early flowers.

Bumblebees and honeybees have also woken up and are in among the crocuses, looking for pollen. Talking about crocuses, did you know that the most expensive food in the world when sold by weight is saffron? Saffron is a deep-orange powder used for flavouring and colouring rice and cakes, and although the flavour it imparts is subtle and wonderful, few of us ever get to taste it. We see the lovely colour it gives to the rice but that's as far as it goes. Very few people can afford to put enough of it in to make it taste. Why is it so expensive? Simply because it is made from the dried orange-red stigmas of the purple crocus (*crocus sativus*) which is very similar to our own spring crocus although it flowers in the autumn. And it takes an awful lot of stigmas (the little pollen-

covered stem in the middle of the flower) to make an ounce
of saffron. In olden times it was grown extensively in Saffron
Walden, Essex, hence the name, and the people who grew it
were known as 'crokers'. Nowadays it is cultivated commer-
cially in Spain, Southern France, Sicily, Iran and Kashmir.
Saffron has been valuable for hundreds of years, and it is
recorded that in Germany in the fifteenth century, two men
were actually burned alive in the marketplace for adulterat-
ing the saffron they sold. Saffron cake is still a favourite
among the people of Cornwall, but although it is beautifully
yellow, I have never been able to taste the flavour of the
saffron in it. After all, the price per ounce of pure saffron
powder is many times higher than for caviar or smoked
salmon or foie gras.

APRIL

NOW at last we can say that spring has arrived, and with it come flocks of summer migrants, all those little birds that flew away to the warmer countries in the south when it began to get cold last October. Most of them go as far as North Africa and don't ask me how they find their way there and back again because that is one of the great mysteries of the world. There are skylarks, greenfinches, goldfinches, whitethroats, willow warblers, golden plovers, blackcaps, swallows, house martins, chiffchaffs and many more besides, and soon after they arrive they pair up and start to build their nests.

This is the month of Easter and the end of another school term. When I was small my mother used always to take all of us six children to Tenby for the Easter holidays. She rented a house known as The Cabin, which was in the Old Harbour, and when the tide was in, the waves broke right up against one wall of the house. We adored Tenby. We had donkey rides on the beach and long walks with the dogs along the top of the cliffs opposite Caldy Island, and there were primroses everywhere. We hunted for winkles on the rocks and carried them home and boiled them and got them out of their shells with bent pins and put them on bread and butter for tea.

Every Easter we made one trip by motorboat to Caldy Island where there is a famous monastery. We were told that the monks had taken the vow of silence and were never allowed to speak even to one another. We would gaze at these silent men in their pale brown robes working in the fields and wonder what it must be like never to say a word except in prayer. I remember thinking even at my tender age how boring their lives must be and wondering whether they were really to be admired for running away from all the troubles and dangers of the world as they appeared to be doing. It would be different, I thought, if they were caring for the sick or doing good works, but they weren't. They simply cultivated their fields and gardens and made perfume from flowers which they sold to the tourists from a little kiosk by the beach. Even when you bought perfume from them, they never spoke.

MAY

NOW at last summer is properly upon us. So is the start of the school summer term. Most boys will be playing cricket, but I don't know what sort of organised games girls play in summer. Rounders? Netball? Tennis, perhaps, if the school is lucky enough to have a court. There is a growing tendency among schools in Britain in recent years to pay less and less attention to organised games and simply to send the children on a run to get rid of their energy. This dismays me because I regard all forms of sport, whether the pupil is good at them or not, as being a most important part of character-building. Sport teaches sportsmanship as well as how to be a good loser, and it teaches a lot of other things besides. Lessons and exams are all very well, but there are other things in life besides being clever and soaking up knowledge.

If I ran a school, I would put up a practice net for golf and give everyone, boys and girls alike, a chance to learn a bit about one of the loveliest games in the world. I started playing golf when I was nine. I had only one old club at first, and I hung up a large piece of sacking on the lawn in our garden and hit golf balls against it. I bought a book on golf and studied it and taught myself. When I was ten, my sister Alfhild and I used often to bike during the holidays to the nearest golf course six miles away with our golf bags slung on our shoulders and then play eighteen holes and bike home again. In those days it cost one pound a year to become a Junior Member, and I believe that most golf clubs even today still allow young people to join for very little money. I actually became pretty good at golf in the end and had a scratch handicap by the time I was seventeen. After that, wherever I was in the world, I played golf for recreation and exercise. I played in Tanganyika, in Kenya, in Egypt, in Sierra Leone, in France, in America and goodness knows where else besides. In Dar es Salaam you had to watch out for cobras. On one course in Kenya you were allowed to lift your ball without penalty from rhinoceros hoof prints. And in Lagos (Nigeria) monkeys used to pelt you with unripe mangoes just as you were about to putt. It was super.

During May, the last of the summer visitors arrive from Africa, the swifts and winchats. Most of the other birds are already sitting on eggs in their beautifully constructed nests, while the earliest nesters of all, the blackbirds and thrushes, have already hatched their young and some have even left the nest and can be seen hopping about under the bushes, calling out to be fed.

May is the month of the cuckoo. Let me tell you about this extraordinary bird and all its nasty habits. First of all, it is a migrant and does not arrive in Europe or the British Isles until April. It stays here until it begins to feel the cold in the early autumn and then it flies south literally for thousands and thousands of miles. It doesn't stop in North Africa like most of the other migrant birds. It goes on and on to tropical Africa or South Africa or sometimes as far away as Asia and New Guinea. It can do this because unlike the swifts and swallows and finches, it is a big strong bird, with a wide wingspread and a long tail.

Everyone living in the countryside knows when the cuckoos start arriving because you cannot help hearing the loud, eerie, almost human call of the male bird. It quite literally says, 'Cuck-koo, cuck-koo', and the voice carries for miles, a strange high-pitched mocking call that seems to be shouting out to all the other birds in the sky that they had better watch out.

And now for its nasty habits. Unlike most other birds, cuckoos do not pair up and stay together. The males and the females fly around separately and they mate indiscriminately here and there, so there are no marriages or family life in cuckooland. When the female is ready to lay her first egg, she nearly always does this on bare ground. Then she picks up the egg in her beak and goes in search of the nest of another bird in which to deposit it. No cuckoo has ever bothered to build its own nest or hatch or feed its young. The female (carrying her egg in her beak) searches the hedgerows until she finds the nest of another bird that already has eggs in it, and she slips her own egg in with the others and flies away and forgets all about it.

Usually, for some unknown reason, cuckoos choose a hedge sparrow's nest. The hedge sparrow's eggs are to me the loveliest of all the eggs in Britain, a pure pale azure blue with no markings on them at all. The cuckoo's egg on the other hand is larger and is a muddy brown colour with darker speckles on it. But the extraordinary thing is that the mother hedge sparrow, when she returns and finds this dirty brown egg lying in her nest among her own blue beauties, does not seem to mind at all and proceeds to sit on it and incubate it together with her own.

Little does she know what is going to happen when all the eggs hatch. There will usually be four or five of her own eggs plus the one cuckoo's egg and when the baby chicks hatch out, the mother and father both feed them all, including the horrid cuckoo chick. Don't forget that the adult cuckoo is a bird three times as big as the hedge sparrow, and therefore the cuckoo chick grows three times as fast as the little sparrows. Then comes the slaughter. The overgrown baby cuckoo proceeds quite literally to push the baby hedge sparrows one by one out of the nest to die, and in the end all that is left is this grotesque, huge, fluffy cuckoo chick filling the entire nest. The craziest thing about all this is that not even then do the hedge sparrow parents seem to notice what has happened, and they go on feeding this murderer, working night and day to bring it enough food to keep it going, until in the end it is big enough to hop out of the nest and fly away without so much as a thank you.

That is why I say that the cuckoo is the nastiest bird in the sky. Too lazy to build its own nest, too lazy to feed its own young, it simply deposits a single killer egg in one nest after the other, then flies on. Each female cuckoo will produce about one dozen eggs per season, in one dozen different nests, and it is curious that they seem nearly always to select a particular breed of bird. In the woods and hedgerows it is, as I have said, usually the poor little hedge sparrow they pick on, but on the moors they frequently choose meadow pipits or tree pipits.

Each female cuckoo laying a dozen or so eggs in a season will therefore kill about sixty babies belonging to other birds by pushing them out of the nest. Not even the worst human being in the world could be as bad as that.

At the beginning of May, you see the beeches and ash trees coming very slowly into leaf. The last trees to produce leaves are the London planes. These are the trees you see lining the streets in towns and cities, and they always look as though half their bark is peeling off. The most beautiful plane trees in London are in Berkeley Square.

In May the hawthorn blossoms make the hedges look as though they are covered in snow and the buttercups are beginning to appear in the fields. As a boy, I used to prise up the little white bulb of the buttercup and chew it. It is frighteningly hot, like mustard. Swallows and house martins are building their crazy mud nests all over the place, the house martins on the vertical walls of buildings, just under the eaves, and the swallows on rafters in outbuildings. We have a pair of swallows that have built their nest in exactly the same place on a wooden beam in the tool shed for the past six years, and it is amazing to me how they fly off thousands of miles to North Africa in the autumn with their young and then six months later they find their way back to the same tool shed at Gipsy House, Great Missenden, Bucks. It's a miracle and the brainiest ornithologists in the world still cannot explain how they do it.

JUNE

A S far as climate goes, June is probably the loveliest month of all, except perhaps for September. If you live by the sea, you will know that the gulls' eggs have nearly all hatched and the cliffs are full of downy chicks. Gulls are not migrants. They stay with us all winter and that is why they are the first of the sea birds to nest and rear their young. Terns on the other hand (you see a lot of arctic terns around the coast of Britain) are summer visitors and most rest a while after their long journey before they start nesting.

Further inland, our island is alive with young birds. Keep your eyes open and you will be astonished at the number of different species you will see. When you hear a bird singing or merely chirping in a tree, look for it and find it and then try to identify it. It is well worthwhile getting a little book with colour plates to help you. There are several good ones on sale, including my favourite, called *The Observer's Book of Birds*, which is small enough to put in your pocket. You can get the same book as a guide to wild flowers and also, I believe, to fungi or mushrooms. But more about mushrooms later.

In the fields you will see great flocks of lapwings (some call them peewits, some plovers) with their enormous wings.

They nest on the ground and if you walk near their chicks they will fly round and round your head, trying to scare you away from their children who are crouching in the grass. This month, on rivers and lakes you will see tiny brown cygnets swimming after their parent swans, and if you go too near them, which I don't advise, the adults will hiss at you and arch their wings, ready to attack.

June is the month of the foxglove, perhaps the most beautiful of all the wild flowers. The foxglove also gives us a drug called digitalis which is valuable to doctors in treating heart conditions. Barley is already standing tall in the fields. Don't confuse it with the other two main cereals, wheat and oats. Barley has long itchy spikes covering the seeds, and if you pick one of these heads and slip it under the sleeve of your jacket or shirt with the long spikes pointing downwards, the head will actually climb all the way up to your shoulder as you walk along swinging your arm.

During this month the tadpoles in the ponds are beginning to sprout tiny arms and legs, and soon they will be turning into small frogs. Be nice to frogs, by the way. They are your friends in the garden. They eat the beastly slugs and never harm your flowers. There is so much beauty in the country-side in June. The lovely pink dog roses are in full bloom along the hedges and wild honeysuckle is plentiful. The honeysuckle flowers are white when they first come out, but they turn orangey-yellow after they have been pollinated by the bees. I'm afraid that if you live in a town you don't see any of these splendid sights, but I have never lived in a town or city in my life and I would hate to do so.

JULY

BEFORE this month is out, the long summer term will be ended and the summer holidays will have begun. For some, the last day of the summer term will be the last day of school for ever, and that is a great moment in one's life. It was like that for me at the end of July 1934. I was not going on to university. I was going first with an exploring expedition to Newfoundland and then to my first job with the Eastern Staff of the Shell Company. But first the summer term at school had to be lived out, and I found an interesting way of making it slightly less tedious. I did this with the help of a motor-bike.

I had bought my motorbike soon after I was sixteen. It was a second-hand Ariel 500cc and it cost me twenty-two pounds. It was a wonderful big powerful machine and when I rode upon it, it gave me an amazing feeling of winged majesty and of independence that I had never known before. Wherever I wished to go, my mighty Ariel would take me. Up to then, I had either had to walk or bicycle or buy a ticket for a bus or a train and it was a slow business. But now all I had to do was sling one leg over the saddle, kick the starter and away I went. I got the same feeling a few years later when I flew single-seater fighter planes in the war. Anyway, my plan now was to enliven the last term at Repton by secretly taking my motorbike with me. So on the first day of that summer term I rode it the hundred and fifty miles from our house in Kent to the village of Wilmington, which is about three miles from Repton. There I left it with a friendly garage owner together with my waders and helmet and goggles and wind jacket. Then I walked the rest of the way to school with my little suitcase.

Sunday afternoons were the only times we had free throughout the school week, and most boys went for long walks in the countryside. But I took no long Sunday afternoon walks during my last term. My walks took me only as far as the garage in Wilmington where my lovely motorbike was hidden. There I would put on my disguise – my waders and helmet and goggles and wind jacket – and go sailing in a state of absolute bliss through the highways and byways of Derbyshire. But the greatest thrill of all was to ride at least once every Sunday afternoon slap through the middle of Repton village, sailing past the pompous prefects and the masters in their gowns and mortarboards. I felt pretty safe with my big goggles covering half of my face, although I will admit that on one famous occasion I got a twist in my stomach when I found myself motoring within a couple of yards of the terrifying figure of the headmaster, Dr Geoffrey Fisher himself, as he strode with purposeful step towards the chapel. He glared at me as I rode past, but I don't think that it would have entered his brainy head for one moment that I was a member of the school. Don't forget that those were the days when schools like mine were merciless places where serious misdemeanours were punished by savage beatings that drew blood from your backside. I am quite sure that if I had ever been caught, that same headmaster would have thrashed me within an inch of my life and would probably have expelled me into the bargain. That is what made it so exciting. I never told anyone, not even my best friend, where I went on my Sunday walks. I had learnt even at that tender age that there are no secrets unless you keep them to yourself, and this was the greatest secret I had ever had to keep in my life so far.

But here we are now in July, in the present, not 1934. So look around you and see what is going on in the wonderful countryside. Some birds, but by no means all, are already beginning to prepare for the great autumn migration. You might catch sight of sand martins gathering in flocks round the reservoirs and lakes. Some of the warblers and white-throats are starting to move south, and the grey plovers and sandpipers are coming down from the Arctic regions on their way to Africa. Not so, of course, the house martins. They are still looking after their second hatching of babies in those crazy mud nests of theirs that cling to vertical walls under the eaves of houses. Towards the end of the month you will notice that buttercups are no longer the commonest field flower, for now the white clover is taking over, and the rowan trees are already beginning to produce berries, although they are not yet red, only orange.

I wonder where you are going on your summer holidays. France perhaps, or Italy or Spain or Greece or better still to Norway or the west coast of Scotland. The coast of Cornwall is lovely too if only you can find a place that doesn't have a million people in it. Preparing to go off on your summer holidays is one of the best moments of the entire year when you are young. Have a great time.

AUGUST

MANY of you will be away on your holidays during the better part of this month. It was the same with me when I was young. Every August was spent in Norway with the family and I have written something about that in my book *Boy*, so I won't go into it again here. But when I became sixteen, I decided it was time to cut the family apron strings and go off somewhere by myself for my August holiday. I chose France. I had twenty-four pounds in my pocket when I crossed the Channel from Dover to Calais and that, in 1933, was just about enough for a two-week holiday plus travel. (A pound in those days was worth almost twenty times as much as it is today. A gallon of petrol, for example, cost two shillings or ten pence.)

From Calais I took a train to Paris and from Paris I got on to an overnight train bound for Marseilles. I had a vague idea that I simply wanted to get to the semi-tropical South of France and see the Mediterranean. I had no other plans. In third class the seats on the train were wooden planks and I sat awake all night long with the fumes of garlic from my fellow passengers drifting around me like poisonous gas. But I shall never forget looking out of the carriage window as dawn broke and seeing my first palm trees. The countryside was

scorched brown by the heat and big date palms were standing in clusters everywhere. It was the palm trees with their
strange bare trunks and a hat of greenery on their heads that
told me I was in a new world.

I got to Marseilles but had no idea where to go next. So I
took a bus that went all along the coastal road towards Monte
Carlo and hoped for the best. By noon I was famished so I got
off the bus at a place called St Jean Cap Ferrat. I was very
mobile because everything I had was in a small suitcase. I
found a café and ate a tureenful of bouillabaisse, which is a
splendid soup made with all sorts of Mediterranean fish and
shellfish, and I finished up in a small yellow hotel on the sea-
front owned by a rather shady Englishman who called himself Major Carruthers. I stayed there for ten days wandering
around by myself and enjoying for the first time in my life the
feeling of being totally alone and doing exactly what I wished
to do from morning till night. Believe me, this is an entirely
new sensation for a young person who has lived all his time
up to then either with a large family or in a large boarding
school. It was my first taste of absolute freedom and my first
glimpse of what it was going to be like to be a grown-up in a
grown-up world.

I travelled back to England the same way I had come, but after I had paid the price of my ticket for the ferry from Calais to Dover, I had not a sou nor a penny left in my pocket. I didn't need a lot, just enough for one more train fare to get me from Dover to my home. On the ferry, I spent half an hour sizing up my fellow passengers, looking for a kind and likely face from whom I could borrow a few shillings. I finally chose a small middle-aged man leaning on the ship's rail smoking a pipe. 'Excuse me, sir,' I said, 'but I have run out of money. If you would lend me ten shillings to get me home, I will promise to send it back to you.' He cocked his head to one side and looked at me with the tiny twinkling wrinkles of a smile around the corners of his eyes. He took out his wallet and handed me a crisp brown ten-shilling note. 'Here you are,' he said. 'Keep it. It's a present. I've got several more in here.' A small gesture, you may say, but it was one that has stuck very clearly in my memory for nearly sixty years.

I find August in England a rather torpid month. The trees and plants have all done their growing for the year and nature is hanging motionless in suspension before sinking slowly into the decline of winter. There is a brownish look to the countryside and the leaves are hanging heavy on the trees. But if it is nothing else, it is the month of the butterfly. Butterflies are lovely things. They do no harm to man himself either by stinging, biting or spreading disease. Nor are they beneficial to man as the silkworm is or the honeybee. The large white or cabbage butterfly is the only one that is a nuisance because it lays eggs on your cabbages and these hatch out into horrid hungry caterpillars.

The life cycle of the butterfly is interesting.

First, the butterfly lays its eggs. It lays them in vast quantities, usually between two and three hundred, but very few of these eggs survive. They are food for countless animals, birds, mice, lizards, spiders and many insects.

Second, the surviving eggs hatch into larvae or caterpillars. These caterpillars gorge themselves on leaves in preparation for the next stage.

Third, the caterpillars turn into pupae or chrysalises which hibernate through the winter and emerge again as butterflies. Thus the cycle is completed.

But there is a snag here. Not all species of butterfly do their hibernating as chrysalises. In some cases, it is the eggs that hibernate, in some it is the caterpillars, and in a few cases, six to be precise, it is the butterflies themselves that hibernate.

You won't believe this, but there is at least one butterfly that is a migrant and that is the red admiral. You know it well. It's the one with the beautiful big eye on its wing. The red admiral breeds in the South of France and this fragile creature actually flies all the way over to Britain in the early summer. There it lays its eggs and these ultimately become more red admirals before the summer is out. But none of them fly back again to France. They die when winter comes.

Butterfly collecting is a fine hobby. To help you, there are several small well-illustrated books available. Once again, I prefer the *Observer's* series.

August is, by the way, the month when young adders are born in heathy, hilly places, and baby grass snakes emerge from their eggs in rotting leaves and old compost heaps. It is the month when hedgehogs have their litters of babies, all born blind and helpless, and I'm afraid it is also the month when wasps come on the warpath, stinging humans in great numbers.

SEPTEMBER

I HAVE always loved this month. As a schoolboy I loved it because it is the Month of the Conker. It is no good knocking down conkers in August because they are still soft and white. But in September, ah, yes, then they are a deep rich brown colour and shining as though they have been polished and that is the time to gather them by the bucketful. I recently wrote a letter to *The Times* newspaper bemoaning the fact that children weren't playing conkers with the same fervour as when I was young. This caused an explosion of angry letters from young enthusiasts all over the country. Nearly one thousand people wrote to me, both boys *and* girls, telling of their love for the sport and of the great contests that were taking place all over the country in the autumn. I received press clippings about The World Conker Championships held at Ashton in Cambridgeshire, and about the All England Conker Championships that were held at Henley. From these letters I learnt that the whole of Britain is still alive with ardent conker players. Many girls wrote to me saying they were just as good as the boys and I was delighted to hear it.

We all know, of course, that a great conker is one that has been stored in a dry place for at least a year. This matures it and makes it rock hard and therefore very formidable. We also know about the short cuts that less dedicated players take to harden their conkers. Some soak them in vinegar for a week. Others bake them in the oven at a low temperature for six hours. But such methods are not for the true conker player. No world-champion conker has ever been produced by short cuts.

I could go on for hours about the best shape to select for a fighting conker – always the flat sharp-edged one, never the big round fellow – and I could talk about the relative merits of using thin and thick string. I could write several pages on the various aiming methods to use and the best swing to adopt when delivering the blow, and the importance of keeping your head still throughout the stroke, and the necessity of a correct stance, but there is no space for all of that here. Suffice it to say that it is a splendid game to play during the winter months and one that requires a cool head and a keen eye.

When I was nine, I made myself a Conker Practising Machine on which I would string up six conkers in a row and work at busting them one after the other. Let's face it, you don't become top class at any sport, be it golf or tennis or snooker or conkers, unless you practise long and hard. The best conker I ever had was a conker 109, and I can still remember that frosty morning in the school playground when my one-o-nine was finally shattered by Perkins's conker 74 in an epic contest that lasted over half an hour. After it, I felt even more shattered than my conker.

But September is also the Month of the Mushroom. You may think it odd that hunting for wild field mushrooms is truly one of my favourite pastimes. Nothing has a more seductive flavour than the fresh wild mushroom gently fried in butter. It is even better with eggs and bacon. And to me the

September

wonder of it is that these treasures are to be had free and for nothing. But you must know where to look. You must know which is a mushroom field and which is not because mushrooms are very mysterious things. They will grow in one field but not in another and there is no explanation for it. But to walk slowly across a green field in the autumn and spot suddenly ahead of you that little pure white dome nestling in the grass, that, I tell you, is exciting. And where there is one, there are usually many more. When you have carefully lifted your mushroom out of the grass and turned it upside down, the delicate pale pink gills are beautiful to behold.

Interestingly enough, it is no crime to pick mushrooms in somebody else's field. The owner cannot prosecute you for stealing. Mushrooms are not like apples or cherries. They have not been cultivated by the owner of the field. They are a freak of nature. Nor can you be prosecuted for trespassing. No farmer can ever prosecute you for trespassing. He can only prosecute you for damaging his property, for breaking down fences or damaging trees or crops. But he *can* ask you to leave his land, and if he does so and is polite about it, then you should go at once. But don't forget to take your mushrooms with you.

Berries are at their best in September. You can still find blackberries and elderberries in the hedges. On the honeysuckle, the berries are brilliant dark red, on the guelder-rose they are scarlet, and on the rowans they are deep orange. Hazelnuts are now ripe brown and ready to be picked, and acorns are dropping down off the oak trees. If you have any apple trees in your garden, some of the early varieties are now ripe to eat. If you examine those horse-chestnut trees from which you knocked down conkers only two weeks before, you will see that next year's sticky buds are already starting to develop, and flies and tiny insects that come too close get stuck on them. More and more trees are beginning to change colour. Even the plane trees, the last to lose their leaves, are turning yellow. The colour of the entire landscape is slowly changing from green to gold.

OCTOBER

THIS, like September, is a lovely month, mild and misty and smelling of ripe apples. We have a small orchard of about five acres at the back of our house and when I first came here nearly forty years ago there were seventy huge old fruit trees filling the whole field. There were apples, pears, cherries and plums and all of them must have been there since the last century. There was so much fruit every autumn that I told all the children in the village they could come in at any time and ask to borrow a ladder and pick what they wanted. They came in droves. Today, old age and storms have finished off many of the trees and there are only about thirty left. Even so, there are still plenty of apples on them, and in October the trees are dripping with big green cookers and rosy eaters, but no children come any more asking to pick. They haven't come for the past ten or fifteen years. I wonder why. Recently, I met a bunch of boys in the lane coming back from school and asked them if they would like to go up the trees and get a basketful of apples. They shook their heads and said, 'Naaw.'

What has happened to these children? I believe they have too much pocket money and prefer to buy crisps and Coke in the shops rather than climb trees for apples. I find this infinitely sad. Boys should *want* to climb trees. They should *want* to build tree-houses. They should *want* to pick apples. Maybe all the crisps and the Coke and the junk food they consume nowadays has made them sluggish.

During this month swarms of migrant birds cross the North Sea from Scandinavia to our shores. Some, like starlings and blackbirds and thrushes and rooks and jackdaws, will stay here for the winter. Others, like the skylarks and goldcrests and finches, will rest before going on south to spend the winter in Africa. Nowadays, the oil rigs in the North Sea provide marvellous observation posts for watching these migrant birds, and men on the rigs often see them wheeling in thousands around the gas flares on their way over from Norway to England. A lot of wood pigeons also cross the North Sea to winter in warmer Britain, and here in the Chiltern Hills where I live, you can see them swarming through the beech woods devouring the ripe nuts of the beech trees which properly are called beech mast.

The lane that goes up the hill past our house is a very old highway and in the Middle Ages used to be the main route used by drovers taking their cattle to Oxford and Banbury markets forty miles to the north. As a result the lane is worn down very deep below the ground so that when you walk in it the fields on either side are only just level with your head. The steep grassy banks to right and left are fully five feet high and on top of each bank grow many varieties of tree. In the space of thirty yards you can see the gnarled old specimens of oak, beech, ash, hornbeam, holly, hawthorn, hazel, briar, ash and alder. They say that the more different trees you can count in a hedge, the older the hedge is. And at this time of the year our hedges are covered with old man's beard and woody nightshade, which curiously enough shows its red berries and its mauve and yellow flowers both at the same time. Hips and haws make splashes of crimson everywhere

and if you chew their red shells they taste quite good. In the grassy banks on either side, an enormous number of different wild flowers and ferns grow. On weekends I see groups of enthusiastic botanists from London hunting for rare specimens. They walk slowly up the lane peering into the banks and calling to one another when they find something interesting. I like these people. I like enthusiasts of any kind.

Ladybirds are now beginning to settle down for the winter in cosy niches and in the corners of windows. There they will sleep until the warmth wakes them up next spring.

NOVEMBER

HERE we are in November and you can really feel the dreaded winter coming on, but with a bit of luck there will be quite a few pleasant days during the month. The beech forests around our way are now a marvellous yellow colour and the larch woods make great splashes of golden flame. The larch is the only English conifer that sheds its needles in winter. Michaelmas daisies are still in full flower and make pink and mauve clusters in the garden. This is the real autumn and the countryside is filled with the beautiful colours of dying leaves.

It is also the middle of what we used to call the Christmas term. I had my first Christmas term away from home in 1924, sixty-six years ago, at boarding school. I was then eight years old. Just for fun, I have been looking through the letters I wrote to my mother at that time. What strikes me most about them is my appalling spelling. Here are a few examples:

I swoped some stamps today...
I got a big serprise...
All the certains were drawen...
It was so funy...

I have lost my jersy...
We had footborl today betwine our school and St Dunstans...
I lost my prair-book in cherch...
We're all getting coalds...
I scord a goal...
We had sosages called pelones. They taist lovely...
Just to make it a bit planer...
They beet us 3-0...
They had a tall gole-keeper...
A man called Mr Mitchell gave us a fine leckture last knight.

Spelling was never my strong point and I'm still not very good at it. But the school did its best. Every word that was spelled wrongly in an essay had to be written out correctly one hundred times after work. I don't know any better way than that of drumming the stuff into you.

November is, of course, the month of fireworks and Guy Fawkes. Oh, how we used to look forward to the fifth of November at boarding school. In these enlightened times no one will believe the things we were allowed to do on that famous night. Each of us eighty small boys aged between seven and twelve were given a box of fireworks (the cost charged up to our parents' bill) and we were all allowed to go out on to the football field in the dark and set them off. The field was seething with boys from seven to twelve years old all setting off their own fireworks with their own matches. Pretty lethal fireworks, too. We had jackie jumpers, Roman candles, crack-bangers, fire-serpents, big bombers, rockets and golden rain. On most of them it said, *Light fuse and stand well away. Do not hold in the hand.* There was precious little supervision over this jamboree, just a master or two wandering casually about, but nothing more. I participated in these great occasions for four years running and the extraordinary thing was that nobody ever got seriously hurt. Naturally there were a few burnt hands here and there, but when that happened you simply went to matron and she put some yellow stuff on the raw place and bandaged it. I know it is not right to subject children to these risks and I wouldn't approve of doing it today. But it also happens to be true that the more risks you allow children to take, the better they learn to take care of themselves. If you never let them take any risks, then I believe they become very prone to injury. Boys should be allowed to climb tall trees and walk along the tops of high walls and dive into the sea from high rocks. It is far better to let them do these things than to keep saying, 'No, Johnny, no. You mustn't. It's dangerous.' The same with girls. I like the type of child who takes risks. Better by far than the one who never does so.

There is a badger's earth in the wood above our house, and this month the badgers are busy digging their deep winter quarters and lining them with dry leaves for warmth. Before November is out, they will have blocked up the entrances to their holes and will sleep the winter through. Like the badgers, the grass snakes are all starting to hibernate, but they are not as domesticated as the badgers. They have no real homes and simply hide themselves among the twisted tree roots underneath the hedges, and quite often they will coil themselves around each other for comfort. For many small animals, the approach of winter means the time to go to sleep until spring arrives again. It would make life a lot more comfortable if we could do the same.

DECEMBER

THIS, as you all know, is the month when two good things happen. The term ends and Christmas comes. For many of you, the whole of December is spent counting the days to Christmas and you can see a stirring among the parents as they begin to perform all the usual rituals like making lists of presents and sending out cards and finally buying the tree itself. By now you will have told them what you are wishing for. I approve very much of children who make their own Christmas cards, and whenever I get one of those I am deeply touched because I know the time and effort that has gone into making it. The cards I hate getting are the ones that have on them a colour photograph of the senders standing proudly somewhere or other surrounded by their offspring. You can be half blinded by the self-satisfaction shining out of their faces as they stare back at you from the card.

Even if you live in a town you can notice several rather unusual birds in your gardens at this time of year. We have a cotoneaster shrub on the wall of our house which is always covered with brilliant red berries in December, and this is a special favourite of a lovely bird called the waxwing. You may swear you have never seen a waxwing and have never even heard the name, but the odds are you *have* seen one several times and simply haven't taken note of it. Waxwings come into Britain in December to escape the freezing weather in Norway and Sweden, but they don't come regularly. Some years they arrive in swarms, other years they don't come at all. If you look in your Bird Book you will see that the waxwing has a marvellous pale brown parrotlike crest on its head. The wings are striped black and white with a flash of scarlet on them, and the tail has a vivid yellow bar at the end of it. The trouble is they are so striking to look at that idiots shoot them for their feathers.

In December the tawny owls in our orchard start hooting like mad all through the night. You will quite often also hear them if you live in a town where they exist by pouncing on starlings and sparrows while they are roosting and fast asleep.

As I write, I am remembering something I did during the Christmas holidays when I was either nine or ten, I can't be sure which. We lived in Kent then, in a fairly large house that had a wide lane and a public footpath running through our land at the back of the house. For Christmas that year I had been given a fine Meccano set as my main present, and I lay in bed that night after the celebrations were over thinking that I must build something with my new Meccano that had never been built before. In the end I decided I would make a device that was capable of 'bombing' from the air the pedestrians using the public footpath across our land.

Briefly my plan was as follows: I would stretch a wire all the way from the high roof of our house to the old garage on the other side of the footpath. Then I would construct from my Meccano a machine that would hang from the wire by a grooved wheel (there was such a wheel in my Meccano box) and this machine would hopefully run down the wire at great speed dropping its bombs on the unwary walkers underneath.

Next morning, filled with the enthusiasm that grips all great inventors, I climbed on to the roof of our house by the skylight and wrapped one end of the long roll of wire around a chimney. I threw the rest of the wire into the garden below and went back down myself through the skylight. I carried the wire across the garden, over the fence, across the footpath, over the next fence and into our land on the other side. I now pulled the wire very tight and fixed it with a big nail to the top of the door of the old garage. The total length of the wire was about one hundred yards. So far so good.

Next I set about constructing from the Meccano my bombing machine, or chariot as I called it. I put the wheel at the top, and then running down from the wheel I made a strong column about two feet long. At the lower end of this column,

I fixed two arms that projected outwards at right angles, one
on either side, and along these arms I suspended five empty
Heinz soup tins. The whole thing looked something like this:

I carried it up to the roof and hung it on the wire. Then I
attached one end of a ball of string to the lower end of the
chariot and let it rip, playing out the string as it went. It was
wonderful. Because the wire sloped steeply from the roof of
the house all the way to the other end, the chariot careered
down the wire at terrific speed, across the garden and over
the footpath, and it didn't stop until it hit the old garage door
on the far side. Great. I was ready to go.

With the string, I hauled the chariot back to the roof. And
now, from a jug I filled all the five soup tins with water. I lay
flat on the roof waiting for a victim. I knew I wouldn't have
to wait long because the footpath was much used by people
taking their dogs for walks in the wood beyond.

Soon two ladies dressed in tweed skirts and jackets and each wearing a hat, came strolling up the path with a revolting little Pekinese dog on a lead. I knew I had to time this carefully, so when they were very nearly but not quite directly under the wire, I let my chariot go. Down she went, making a wonderful screeching-humming noise as the metal wheel ran down the wire and the string ran through my fingers at great speed. Bombing from a height is never easy. I had to guess when my chariot was directly over the target, and when that moment came, I jerked the string. The chariot stopped dead and the tins swung upside down and all the water tipped out. The ladies, who had halted and looked up on hearing the rushing noise of my chariot overhead, caught the cascade of water full in their faces. It was tremendous. A bull's-eye first time. The women screamed. I lay flat on the roof so as not to be seen, peering over the edge, and I saw the women shouting and waving their arms. Then they came marching straight into our garden through the gate at the back and crossed the garden and hammered on the door. I nipped down smartly through the skylight and did a bunk.

Later on, at lunch, my mother fixed me with a steely eye and told me she was confiscating my Meccano set for the rest of the holidays. But for days afterwards I experienced the pleasant warm glow that comes to all of us when we have brought off a major triumph.

I hope you all have a lovely Christmas and a super holiday.

First published 1993
1 3 5 7 9 10 8 6 4 2

Text copyright © Felicity Dahl and the other
Executors of the Estate of Roald Dahl 1991
Illustrations copyright © Quentin Blake 1993

This edition first published in the United Kingdom in 1993 by
Jonathan Cape Limited
Random House, 20 Vauxhall Bridge Road, London SW1V 2SA

First published in THE DAHL DIARY 1992, Puffin Books

Random House Australia (Pty) Limited
20 Alfred Street, Milsons Point, Sydney
New South Wales 2061, Australia

Random House New Zealand Limited
18 Poland Road, Glenfield
Auckland 10, New Zealand

Random House South Africa (Pty) Limited
PO Box 337, Bergvlei, South Africa

Random House UK Limited Reg. No. 954009

A CIP catalogue record for this book
is available from the British Library

ISBN 0 224 03647 5

Typeset in Garamond by Creative Text Ltd
Printed and bound in Singapore by Tien Wah Press (Pte) Ltd